LEARN TO PLAY IN THE ORCHESTRA

By RALPH MATESKY

CONTENTS

TITLE (COMPOSER)	STRING BOOK PAGE	SCORE BOOK PAGE	CORRELATES TO "LEARN TO PLAY A STRINGED INSTRUMENT"	
			LESSON	SEQUENCE
1. Trumpet Tune (H. Purcell)	4	4	26	1
2. Musette (J.S. Bach)	4	5	26	2
3. Happy Dance (L. Mozart)	5	6	26	3
4. Folk Dance (L. van Beethoven)	6	8	26	4
5. Swedish Folk Song	6	9	27	1
6. Slow Song (W. A. Mozart)	7	10	27	2
7. French Folk Song	7	11	27	3
8. Drink to Me Only With Thine Eyes (English Folk Song)	8	12	27	4
9. Christmas Song (Carol)	9	14	27	5
10. Dance Tune (B. Bartok)	9	15	27	6
11. Barcarolle (C. Czerny)	10	16	27	7
12. March in the Style of Corelli (R. Matesky)	11	18	27	8
13. Tomahawk! (R. Matesky)	14	22	28	1
14. Austrian Folk Song (C. Czerny)	15	24	28	2
15. Mary and Joseph (Christmas Song)	15	25	31	1
16. Sweet Betsy from Pike (American Folk Song)	16	26	31	2
17. Minuet in the Style of Haydn (R. Matesky)	16	28	31	3
18. Theme from Sonata in G Major, Op. 96 (L. van Beethoven)	17	30	35	1
19. La Chasse [The Chase] (N. Paganini)	18	32	36	1
20. Spanish Carol	19	34	37	1
21. Holy, Holy, Holy (J. Dykes)	19	36	38	1
22. Song of Brotherhood [from 9th Symphony] (L. van Beethoven)	20	37	38	2
23. Pizzicato Pete (R. Matesky)	20	38	40	1
24. Simple Hymn (R. Matesky)	21	40	41	1
25. Square Dance (R. Matesky)	21	41	41	2
26. German Lullaby (German Folk Song)	22	44	41	3
27. Fantastic Melody [from Fantasie-Impromptu] (F. Chopin)	23	46	41	4
28. Men of Harlech (Welsh Folk Song)	24	48	41	5

INSTRUMENTATION

- SCORE & PIANO ACCOMPANIMENT
- VIOLIN I
- VIOLIN II
- VIOLAS I & II
- CELLO
- BASS

D1247342

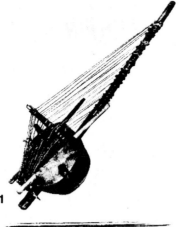

Harp-lute type instrument Senegambia (Africa)

2

1

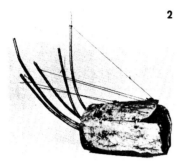

African harp, Nonga (East Africa)

3

Tromba Marina

Trumscheit – single string Bass Viol. Note bow and manner of fingering.

5

Left – *Very old Yugoslav one-stringed instrument. Notice bow! Also very ornate scroll.* Middle – *Persian 3 string Spike-fiddle (Kamang)* Right – *Very old Mongolian one-stringed instrument. Notice bow and its similarity to modern German Bass bow.*

7   **8**

9

Left – *Viola da Gamba (6 stgs) Bavarian, about 1550.* Right – *Small Viol (Lira da Braccin) Verona, 1511.* Below – *Monteverdi with his Bass Viol. Note Viola da Braccia on wall, (about 1600).*

A SHORT HISTORY OF STRINGED INSTRUMENTS

Stringed instruments are among the oldest known to man. It is very difficult to state exactly when or where stringed instruments were first made and played, but authorities generally agree that they started in Asia. Mention of bowed stringed instruments has been found in ancient Sanskrit writings. Sanskrit is a language that dates back to 150 A.D. Further, if we recall the stories in the bible, there are many, many references to cymbals, trumpets, drums, harps, etc., so music and instruments go back many thousands of years.

There are two main kinds of stringed instruments: (1) those that are plucked, like the harp, guitar, lute; and, (2) those that are played with a bow, like the violin, viola, violoncello and string bass. Since the stringed instruments studied in your classes and those in the modern orchestra are mostly the bowed type, we will talk only about them. (See 1 and 2)

As we know them today, stringed instruments reached their perfected shapes and tonal qualities about the year 1650 (almost 350 years ago), in Italy. Germany and France produced fine makers shortly thereafter. Many wonderful old instruments dating from this time are still in use by string players today, but a great many have been lost due to wars, natural catastrophes or just plain carelessness on the part of those who used them. However, it may be surprising to learn that the ancestors of stringed instruments date all the way back to 500 B.C. (almost 2500 years ago) and can be found in nearly all older civilizations including China, Japan, India, Egypt, Africa and many others. Here are some pictures of the very, very old stringed instruments. Notice that in many cases they are simple, one-stringed instruments, with some kind of sounding box attached. But see also how beautiful some of them are – especially the oriental stringed instruments – and, in certain cases, how many strings some of them have. (See 3, 4, 5 and 6)

As time went on these instruments developed in Europe from about 1400-1600 into a family called the VIOLONS or VIOLS. These were divided into arm-instruments (BRACCIA) [*Brah-chee-yah*]; and leg-instruments (GAMBA) [*Gahm-bah*]. The smaller ones were held in the arm, while the larger ones were held by the legs. The smaller ones sounded higher and lighter because the strings were shorter and the bodies smaller; the larger ones sounded lower and deeper because their strings were longer and the bodies larger. Notice the shape of the sound holes on the tops of these old viols, their graceful shapes, and the beautiful decorations on them — especially on the scrolls (heads). Notice also that they have as few as one string and as many as seven strings with seven additional sympathetic — or helping-the-sound, strings. (See 7, 8 and 9)

Toward the end of the 16th century, about 1575, the violons were displaced by the violin family. The earliest violin was called the REBEC or REBAB and looked like those in photos 10 and 11.

It was first used in the early 11th and 12th centuries, became less important when the violon family was developed, then returned to become the string family of violins we know today.

Notice how the BOWS of all the older instruments were curved *out* and look almost like the hunting bow. It is very possible that the "twang" of the hunter's bow was one of the first musical sounds made by primitive man. With bows of different sizes, and lengths, the pitch (sound) would change; and so it is not hard to imagine the very first beginnings of the HARP coming from the different sounds of these different bow strings. (See 12 and 13)

The chief differences between VIOLS and VIOLINS are: (1) viols were weak and thin in tone; violins are much stronger and richer, (2) viols were built in many different shapes, sizes and with varying numbers of strings tuned in different ways; violins were built more evenly and scientifically, with only four strings, tuned in 5ths (five notes apart). However, one of these old viols is still used today in the string family — it is the double bass and is the only original descendant of the old violon family. It still has a flat back, sloping shoulders, high bridge and deep-set ribs. The violin family has arched top and back, rounded shoulders, a flatter bridge, and ribs which are not set quite so deeply into the sides of the instrument. Also, the sound holes, or "*f*" holes, are shaped and placed differently than the crescent holes of the viols. (See 14 and 15)

Left — *Viols of the 16th Century. Different shapes & sizes. Note curved bows. (Painting by Raphael)*

Below — *Rebec (forerunner of violin) and Lute.*

Right — *Musical bow from Kilimanjaro region in East Africa.*
Below — *Musical bow from Medje tribe in Congo, Africa.*

14

Above — *Nicolo Amati violin (17th Century). Note ornamentation. Not many great violins were made this way.*

15

Right — *Jan Kubelik's (famous violinist) Stradivarius violin (1715). It is called the "Emperor".*

HENRY PURCELL (c. 1659-1695) Purcell was one of England's greatest composers. Even though he lived but 36 years, he created many fine works. He was most successful in setting of the English language to music in his songs. Few composers have achieved his great output, variety, and success in so short a life span.

Trumpet Tune

HENRY PURCELL
Arr. R. Matesky

Allegro

JOHANN SEBASTIAN BACH (1685-1750) J. S. Bach was not only one of the world's greatest composers, but he was also a great teacher, a remarkable performer and a wonderful person. He was always interested in his family — he married twice and had a total of twenty children — taught not only his children but also his wives to sing and play and wrote many exercises and pieces for them as well as for his other students. These works were not only fine teaching pieces but were also masterpieces because of Bach's genius. He was a very religious and modest man. Late in his life one of his admirers asked him how he was able to write so much great music and accomplish so much in so many ways. His answer is a lesson for all of us: "If you would work as long and as hard as I, you, too, could achieve this."

Musette

J.S. BACH
Arr. R. Matesky

Allegro

LEOPOLD MOZART (1719-1787) Not only must Leopold Mozart be credited for being the father of and teacher of Wolfgang Amadeus Mozart, but he was an excellent musician, author and teacher. To him we owe the honor for being one of the first to write a book on violin playing. It is a fine book and tells us much about the way the violin was played (and taught) in those days. Leopold also wrote a considerable amount of music for violin, orchestra and piano. He was a good father and the letters between him and his children indicate love and respect for each other, even though they didn't always agree on things.

Happy Dance

The Mozart family: "Nannerl", Wolf-gang and Leopold (father).

LEOPOLD MOZART
Arr. and adapted R. Matesky

Allegro

LUDWIG van BEETHOVEN (1770-1827) Considered by many to be the greatest composer of all, Ludwig was born on December 17, 1770 at Bonn, Germany. Both his father and grandfather were musical, but there were no great family musicians before him or after him. He was, like W. A. Mozart, a child prodigy on the piano and violin at the age of nine. His first composition was published when he was only ten years old. He played for Mozart in Vienna when he was 14 years old and astonished him. Mozart gave him a few composition lessons, but Beethoven had to return to Bonn and help support his family. Later, Beethoven also took a few lessons with Joseph Haydn and, as he grew to manhood, became famous and successful as a highly respected composer and pianist. But fate had a terrible blow in store for him — he was growing deaf and from the age of about 28 he suffered much from this illness.

Beethoven stood for the rights of man and was a great champion of liberty. His compositions glorify man's ideals and God. Beethoven was not only a great composer, he was also a great man.

Folk Dance

L. van BEETHOVEN
Adapted and arr. R. Matesky

Swedish Folk Song

Arr. R. Matesky

WOLFGANG AMADEUS MOZART (1756-1791) One of the greatest composers, Wolfgang was the darling of audiences and royalty in all of Europe when he was only seven years old. He is credited with writing his first piece at the age of four. He toured Europe as a child prodigy on the piano and violin. His compositions include many, many masterpieces. There are over 600 catalogued works and he was only 36 years old when he died. His life, though full of joy as a child and as a young man, was not too happy after he married, since he was constantly in financial trouble. When he died he was buried in an unmarked grave in Vienna.

Slow Song

WOLFGANG A. MOZART
Arr. R. Matesky

There are countless lovely folk songs from France. This one is delightful. The melody has been given to Part II of the violins and violas in this arrangement.

French Folk Song

Arr. R. Matesky

Drink to Me Only With Thine Eyes is one of the best known and best loved of all English folk melodies. It is a solo for Part II of the violins and violas in this setting. Be sure to bring out the melody.

Drink To Me Only With Thine Eyes

English Folk Song
Arr. R. Matesky

This melody is sometimes called "Oh, Come, Little Children." It is one of the oldest and nicest of Christmas carols.

Christmas Song

Traditional
Arr. R. Matesky

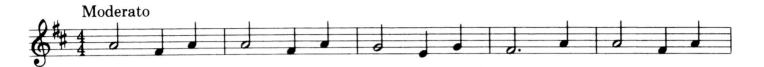

BELA BARTOK (1881-1945) Bela Bartok is one of the greatest contemporary composers. He was born in Hungary and worked with Kodaly in studying Hungarian folk music for many years. Hundreds of songs were recorded by both of these great composers and teachers. Bartok used much folk music in his compositions and his Mikrocosmos is a masterpiece of short teaching pieces for the piano in modern style.

He came to New York in 1940 and struggled to earn a living. He died in 1945 and dedicated his last work, the third piano concerto, to his wife. Even today, it is sad to realize that we do not recognize our greatest living composers. It wasn't until after 1945 that Bartok was generally recognized for his greatness.

Dance Tune

B. BARTOK
Arr. R. Matesky

A barcarolle is a boat song and is usually a smooth, rolling melody. This one, in thirds—that is, three notes apart—moves easily and gracefully as though you were rowing on the water. It will require good bowing and fingering to play this well.

Barcarolle

(in Thirds)

C. CZERNY
Arr. R. Matesky

Andantino

ARCHANGELO CORELLI (1653-1713) Corelli was a great Italian violinist, teacher and composer. He had many fine students. He wrote exclusively for strings and developed the art of violin playing to a high degree in his time. He, with Tartini, was responsible for changing the shape of the outward curved bow to a shape which led Francois Tourte about 35 years later to develop the modern bow. He was a master of beautiful melody and harmony. This piece is composed in the harmonic style of Corelli. Notice the interesting combinations of sound.

March in the Style of Corelli

R. MATESKY

An instrument maker's workshop (late 18th century).

GREAT VIOLIN MAKERS

Some of the greatest makers of the modern violin family of stringed instruments
are listed below. Notice how many of them are from Italy.

NAME	DATE	COUNTRY	NOTES

The Amati (Ah-*mah*-tee) Family
    Andreas Amati
    Antonio Amati
    Girolamo (Hieronymo) Amati
    Nicolo Amati
	
	1535-1611
	1555-1649
	1556-1630
	1596-1684
		Italy	A good many of the instruments of these makers are still played. Very fine; very expensive.

Giovanni Maggini (Gee-oh-*vahn*-ee Mah-*jeen*-ee)	1580-1632	Italy	Very few of his instruments left.
Antonio Stradivarius (An-*tohn*-ee-oh Strad-i-*vair*-ee-us)	1644-1737	Italy	One of the two greatest makers. There are quite a few of his masterpieces available, but the cost is very, very high.
The Testore Family (6 makers) (Tes-*tohr*-ay)	1660-1770	Italy	Although there are quite a few of these instruments available, they are not usually in healthy condition. Prices are high.
The Gagliano (Gah-lee-*ah*-noh) Family There were 16 makers in this family	1660-1886	Italy	There are many, many examples of the instruments of this family. Many are very fine. Priced quite high.

The Guarnerius (Gwar-*nair*-ee-us) Family
    There were 9 makers in this family but
    the most famous were:
                Andreas
                Peter
                Joseph (del Gesu)
	
	1626-1698
	1695-1762
	1698-1744
		Italy	The most famous maker was Joseph (del Gesu) who ranks with Stradivarius. His instruments are among the greatest in the world. Very expensive.

The Tononi Family (7 makers)	1670-1768	Italy	Excellent makers whose instruments are rather high priced.
The Ruggieri (Roo-gee-*air*-ee) Family (3 makers)	1645-1735	Italy	Excellent makers whose instruments are expensive. Not too many available.
The Guadagnini (Gwad-ah-*nee*-nee) Family (17 makers)	1697-1942	Italy	The most famous of these was J. B. Guadagnini whose instruments are wonderful and very costly. This is the longest family line in violin making.
Carlo Bergonzi	1676-1747	Italy	A pupil of Stradivarius. Great maker. Costly instruments. Not too many available.
Jakob Stainer (*Sty*-ner)	1621-1683	Germany	The most famous of the early German makers. Quite a few of his instruments are still available although there are many thousands of imitations.
Lorenzo Storioni (Stor-ee-*oh*-nee)	1751-1801	Italy	A fine maker. Rather expensive instruments. Quite a few available.
G. F. Pressenda	1777-1854	Italy	Considered one of the best of the more "modern" Italian makers. His instruments are rapidly rising in cost.
G. A. Rocca (*Roh*-kah)	1807-1865	Italy	An excellent maker.

There are hundreds of other lesser known but fine makers in Italy, France and Germany as well as in England and other countries. Some of the great French instrument makers include N. Lupot (Loo-poh) and G. B. Vuillaume (Vee-yawm), whose work ranks with the finest Italian makers.

VIOLIN

VIOLA

GREAT BOW MAKERS

There are the great bow-makers of history and among these are Francois Tourte (Toort) (French) (1747-1835) who is called the inventor and perfector of the modern bow along with his older brother, Xavier. He changed the curve of the bow.

Other great French bow makers include Pecatte, Sartory, Semon, Vuillaume, Pageot, Pique, Henri, Lamy. Some of the great English bow makers were Dodd, Tubbs and Hill. German bow makers of fame are Nurnberger, Schuster and Pfretzchner.

It is interesting to discover that the Italians dominated the stringed instrument-making art, while the French dominated the bow-making art.

Here is a picture of the VIOLIN FAMILY with important information about each member:

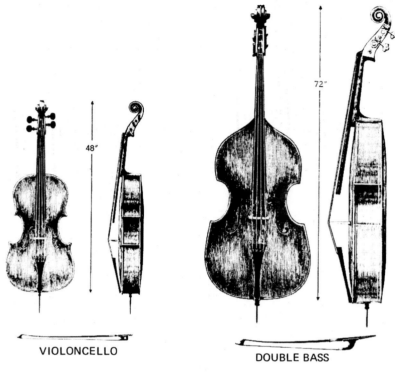

VIOLONCELLO

DOUBLE BASS

THE VIOLIN FAMILY

The violin, smallest and highest pitched, gives the family its name.

The viola, between the violin and violoncello, has a pitch a fifth below that of the violin.

The violoncello, third member in size and pitch, superseded the viola da gamba in the 18th century; it is really a bass violin.

The double bass, sole survivor of the viol type of instrument, retains many of its characteristics.

The bows used with these instruments are of nearly the same length, but vary in weight and construction.

Not shown is the French Bass Bow which is very similar to the Cello Bow, but heavier in weight. It is held and played like the cello bow.

The modern symphony orchestra uses the stringed instrument family in the following usual seating plan and numbers:

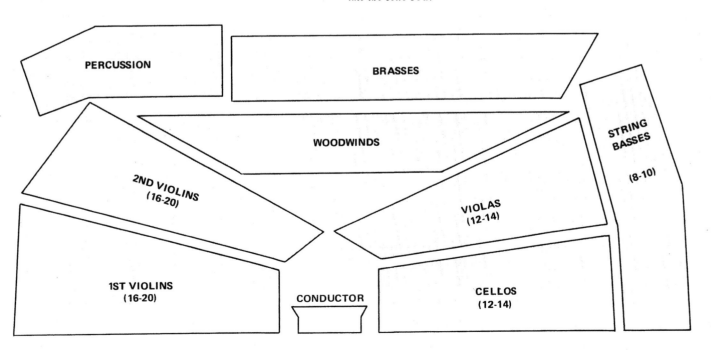

PERCUSSION

BRASSES

WOODWINDS

STRING BASSES (8-10)

2ND VIOLINS (16-20)

VIOLAS (12-14)

1ST VIOLINS (16-20)

CONDUCTOR

CELLOS (12-14)

This is a piece written in the style of American Indian music. It has a strong beat and should be played with much vigor. The cello and bass should play in the style of tom-tom drums.

Tomahawk!

R. MATESKY

With a strong beat

CARL CZERNY (1791-1857) Czerny was born in Vienna and studied with his own father. At the age of nine he was an accomplished pianist and began his teaching career at the age of 14. He also studied piano and composition with Beethoven and was one of his best friends. He wrote over 1000 compositions, but he is best remembered for his works for piano, especially his studies which remain today as a basic source of technical and musical development for every piano student.

Austrian Folk Song

C. CZERNY
Adapted and Arr. R. Matesky

This is one of the loveliest old Christmas carols. Observe how the melody changes from Part I to Part II in the ninth measure, of the violins and violas. Play it with great smoothness (legato).

Mary and Joseph

Christmas Song

Arr. R. Matesky

This is a favorite old American song in waltz time. It has been arranged as a solo for the cellos. Be sure the accompaniment is not too loud for the solo.

Sweet Betsy from Pike

Cello Solo

American Folk Tune
Arr. R. Matesky

FRANZ JOSEPH HAYDN (1732-1809) "Papa" Haydn has been called the father of the symphony form. He composed 104 symphonies! He also composed many more works in other forms.

Haydn was born at Rohrau, Austria just bordering on Hungary. He studied music at a very early age and sang, and played the violin and harpsichord very well. By 1756 when he was 24 years old, he was famous as a teacher and composer. In 1781-82, Haydn and Mozart became friends and Mozart said: "It was from Haydn that I first learned to write a quartet." Haydn said about Mozart: "He is the greatest composer I know either by name or personally." And Haydn also learned some things from Mozart such as a richer style and fuller orchestral mastery.

During the year that Napoleon invaded Austria (1809) and occupied Vienna, Haydn died at the age of 77. Many of the French soldiers followed the funeral procession in admiration of Haydn's work.

This piece was written in the style of a minuet from an early symphony or quartet by Haydn.

Minuet in the Style of Haydn

R. MATESKY

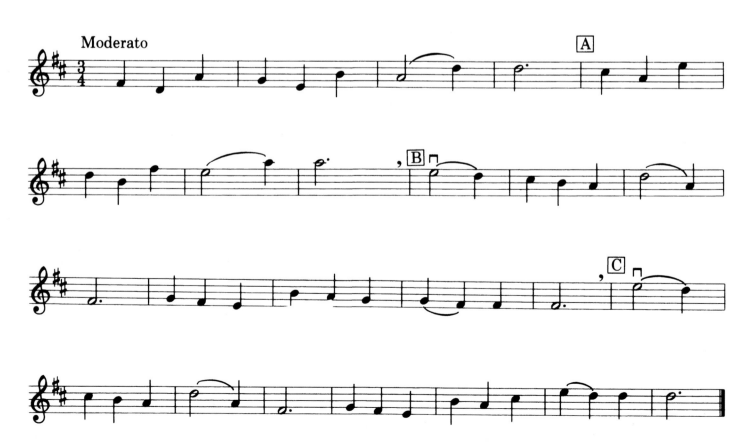

This sonata for violin and piano is one of Beethoven's most beautiful. The melody used in this arrangement is the theme from the last movement of the sonata. It is another example of Beethoven's genius for beautiful melody.

Theme from Sonata in G Major

BEETHOVEN, Op. 96
Arr. R. Matesky

NICOLO PAGANINI (1784-1840) One of the most original geniuses of all time, Paganini, was born in Genoa, Italy on February 14, 1784. He studied violin with his father and practiced so long and so well that he created a sensation when he was only nine years old. He wrote violin music of such daring, originality and difficulty, that only he could play it well. He mystified audiences with his astounding technique and startling effects. To this day his music presents the utmost challenge to violinists. He was very successful in his career —especially in his later days—and left a fortune to his heirs and his great violin, a magnificent Guarnerius del Gesu, to the city of Genoa, where it is now a municipal treasure.

La Chasse

The Chase

N. PAGANINI
Arr. R. Matesky

Nicolo Paganini (about 1820) — one of the greatest violinists of all time.

A unique and especially attractive carol from Spain. Notice the modal quality and interesting rhythm. Play the staccato notes very crisply.

Spanish Carol

Arr. R. Matesky

This is one of the great hymns, traditional in many denominational hymn books. John Dykes was one of the fine church composers.

Holy, Holy, Holy

J. DYKES
Arr. R. Matesky

This theme is from the last—the ninth—symphony by Beethoven, the only one using a chorus and vocal soloists. This is Beethoven's masterpiece to the joy of living and the brotherhood of man. It was written in 1826, one year before his death. The theme is simple, strong and noble. It is the main idea of the final, choral movement of the symphony. People all over the world know and love it.

Song of Brotherhood

from 9th Symphony

L. van BEETHOVEN
Arr. R. Matesky

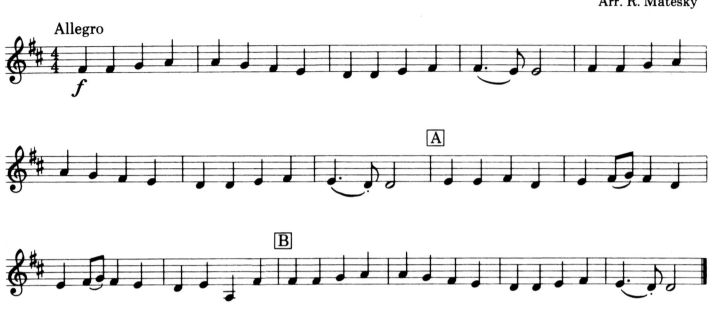

This is a fun-piece using pizzicato. Don't hurry it when you play or practice it. If your finger gets sore from plucking too much, try playing it with your bow until all the notes are learned.

Pizzicato Pete

R. MATESKY

This is a chorale, or church piece. Work for pure intonation, clear tone and perfect harmony. Save your bow on the long notes. Watch the dynamics (mf, f, mp, <, etc.).

Simple Hymn

R. MATESKY

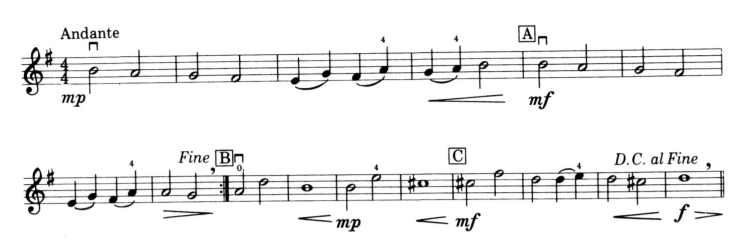

Written in the form and style of the old western dance, this piece should be played as fast as possible with a good, clear, bow stroke. Watch the string crossings, use your whole arm on the bow stroke, and keep the wrist free. Don't press too hard, or you'll spoil your tone.

Square Dance

R. MATESKY

Another well known German folk song. Work for a fine and pure tone when crossing strings.

German Lullaby

Adapted R. Matesky

FREDERIC CHOPIN (1810-1849) Chopin is considered Poland's foremost composer. He was a great pianist and created entirely new styles and color in piano playing. His mother was Polish and his father was French. Chopin reflected the best qualities of both backgrounds in his music. In 1829 he went to Vienna where he gave his first professional concerts as a pianist. He had great success there and two years later went to Paris where he spent most of his life. He suffered from a lung disease and went to the Island of Majorca (off Spain) to recover. His dear friend, Mme. Dudevant, known by her literary name of "George Sand," helped him recover his health. Eventually, however, he died of this illness.

His musical creations were nearly all devoted to the piano. This theme from his Fantasy-Impromptu is one of his best known works.

Fantastic Melody

from Fantasie-Impromptu

F. CHOPIN
Arr. R. Matesky

Men of Harlech

Welsh Folk Song
Arr. R. Matesky